CHICKEN DINNERS

CHICKEN DINNERS

THE BEST CHICKEN DISHES

This edition published by Parragon Books Ltd in 2014 distributed by

Parragon Inc.
440 Park Avenue South, 13th Floor
New York, NY 10016
www.parragon.com/lovefood

LOVE FOOD is an imprint of Parragon Books Ltd

ISBN 978-1-4723-2991-2

Printed in China

New recipes written by Beverly Le Blanc
Introduction and incidental text written by Anne Sheasby
New photography by Clive Streeter
New home economy by Teresa Goldfinch
Additional design by Siân Williams
Internal illustrations by Nicola O'Byrne and Julie Ingham

Notes for the Reader
This book uses standard kitchen measuring spoons and cups. All spoon and cup measurements are level unless
otherwise indicated. Unless otherwise stated, milk is assumed to be whole, eggs are large, individual vegetables
are medium, and pepper is freshly ground black pepper. Unless otherwise stated, all root vegetables should be
peeled prior to using.

Garnishes, decorations, and serving suggestions are all optional and not necessarily included in the recipe
ingredients or method. The times given are only an approximate guide. Preparation times differ according to the
techniques used by different people and the cooking times may also vary from those given. Optional ingredients,
variations, or serving suggestions have not been included in the time calculations.

Picture acknowledgments
The publisher would like to thank the following for the permission to reproduce copyright material: cover
illustration courtesy of iStock.

CONTENTS

PECKING ORDER

Chicken is the most readily available of all poultry and probably the most widely eaten, too. Chicken is bred for its meat and eggs and can be obtained all year round. Depending on the type of chicken you buy and whether you buy a whole bird or chicken parts or pieces, it can also be an economical choice.

Chicken is versatile in cooking and is used in many different dishes across the world. It is easy to cook and is suitable for a wide variety of cooking methods, including roasting, baking, pan-frying, stir-frying, deep-frying, grilling, broiling, poaching, steaming, pot-roasting, casseroling, and braising.

Chicken breast meat is lean and pale with a fine texture and a delicate flavor. It tends to cook more quickly than the darker leg meat, which has a denser texture and is more flavorful. Small, tender chicken livers are delicately flavored and are used to make dishes such as pâtés and terrines. The giblets (usually comprising the neck, gizzard, liver, heart, and sometimes kidney) can be used to make stock or gravy.

Fresh or frozen raw chicken is available, sold either as whole, oven-ready birds or as chicken parts (including breasts on the bone, skinless, boneless breasts, whole legs, thighs, drumsticks and wings), chicken strips, or ground chicken. Prepared raw chicken, such as marinated, seasoned, or coated whole birds or parts, are also available for you to cook at home.

There are different types and breeds of chicken and most supermarkets, butchers, farm shops, and farmers' markets offer a good range of chicken to buy. If you can, choose free-range or organic birds because they will have had a better upbringing to higher welfare standards, they are a more ethical and healthy choice and their flavor is often superior, but they are also more expensive.

Ideally, buy the best-quality chicken that you can afford, preferably grade A, from a trusted supplier (who should be able to tell you where the chicken came from and how it was reared). Intensively reared chickens are cheaper, but the quality, flavor, and texture of the meat can be affected by the way the birds are bred or factory-farmed and are usually inferior as a consequence of this.

Chicken is an excellent source of protein and provides some vitamins and minerals, including the B vitamins and selenium. Chicken is also low in fat and is lower in saturated fat than many other meats, especially when the skin is removed. The skin can be left on during cooking to help keep the chicken moist and add flavor, then you can remove it before serving, if you like.

APPETIZERS, SNACKS & SIDES

CHICKEN CROSTINI

SERVES: 4   **PREP TIME: 15 MINS**   **COOK TIME: 10 MINS**

INGREDIENTS

12 slices of French bread
or rustic bread

¼ cup olive oil

2 garlic cloves, chopped

2 tablespoons finely chopped
fresh oregano, plus extra to
garnish

4 ounces cold, roasted chicken,
cut into thin slices

4 tomatoes, sliced

12 thin slices of goat cheese

12 black ripe olives,
pitted and chopped

salt and pepper, to taste

1. Preheat the oven to 350°F and the broiler to medium. Put the bread under the preheated broiler and lightly toast on both sides.

2. Meanwhile, pour the oil into a bowl and add the garlic and oregano. Season with salt and pepper and mix well. Remove the toasted bread slices from the broiler and spoon a little of the oil mixture on one side.

3. Place the bread slices, oiled sides up, on a baking sheet. Put some of the sliced chicken on top of each one, followed by a slice of tomato. Divide the slices of goat cheese among them, then top with the olives.

4. Drizzle with the remaining oil mixture and transfer to the preheated oven. Bake for about 5 minutes, or until the cheese is golden and starting to melt. Garnish with oregano and serve immediately.

CHICKEN SALAD CUPS

Chicken salad is great for picnics and is easily assembled. Here, the salad is served in dainty toast cups, but it can also be spread on slices of soft bread and turned into a sandwich.

MAKES: 20 FILLED TOAST CUPS

PREP TIME: 20–25 MINS

COOK TIME: 10–15 MINS PLUS COOLING

INGREDIENTS

1 loaf white bread, thinly sliced

unsalted butter or margarine, softened

1½ cups finely chopped, cooked chicken

3 celery stalks, minced

⅓ cup finely chopped pecans, toasted

1 teaspoon honey mustard

1 teaspoon lemon juice

mayonnaise

salt and pepper, to taste

1. Preheat the oven to 325°F. Roll the bread slices flat with a rolling pin. Lightly butter one side of each slice of bread. Cut a circle from each slice, using a small cookie cutter. Press the circles into ramekins (individual ceramic dishes), buttered side up. Bake in the preheated oven for 10–15 minutes, or until lightly browned. Remove from the ramekins and cool completely.

2. Combine the chicken, celery, pecans, honey mustard, and lemon juice in a bowl stirring gently. Add enough mayonnaise to moisten the chicken mixture. Season with salt and pepper. Fill the toast cups with the chicken mixture and serve immediately.

CRISPY CHICKEN & HAM CROQUETTES

These croquettes make a great appetizer or a snack at any time of day. Serve with garlic mayonnaise or another dipping sauce of your choice.

MAKES: 8

PREP TIME: 20 MINS PLUS CHILLING

COOK TIME: 20–25 MINS

INGREDIENTS

¼ cup olive oil

¼ cup all-purpose flour

1 cup milk

1 cup cooked chicken pieces, minced

2 ounces prosciutto, finely chopped

1 tablespoon chopped fresh flat-leaf parsley

small pinch of freshly grated nutmeg

1 egg, beaten

2 slices day-old white bread crumbs

sunflower oil, for deep-frying

salt and pepper, to taste

garlic mayonnaise, to serve

1. Heat the olive oil in a saucepan over medium heat. Stir in the flour to form a paste and cook gently for 1 minute, stirring constantly.

2. Remove the pan from the heat and gradually stir in the milk until smooth. Return to the heat and slowly bring to a boil, stirring constantly, until the mixture boils and begins to thicken.

3. Remove the pan from the heat, add the chicken, and beat until the mixture is smooth. Add the prosciutto, parsley, and nutmeg and mix well. Season with salt and pepper.

4. Spread the chicken mixture in a dish and let stand for 30 minutes, until cool, then cover and chill in the refrigerator for 2–3 hours or overnight.

5. Divide the chicken mixture into eight portions. Use wet hands to form each portion into a cylindrical shape.

6. Pour the beaten egg onto a plate and put the bread crumbs on a separate plate. Dip the croquettes, one at a time, in the beaten egg, then roll in the bread crumbs to coat. Chill in the refrigerator for at least 1 hour.

7. Heat enough sunflower oil for deep-frying in a large saucepan or deep fryer to 350–375°F, or until a cube of bread browns in 30 seconds. Add the croquettes and deep-fry for 5–10 minutes, or until golden brown and crisp.

8. Remove the croquettes with a slotted spoon and drain well on paper towels.

9. Serve piping hot, along with garlic mayonnaise for dipping.

QUICK CHICKEN NACHOS

Nachos are always a big hit with all the family. The addition of chicken to this favorite makes for a tasty twist on the classic version using refried beans.

SERVES: 4　　　　**PREP TIME: 10 MINS**　　　　**COOK TIME: 10–15 MINS**

INGREDIENTS

4 cups salted tortilla chips

1 cup shredded, cooked chicken

¾ cup shredded American cheese or cheddar cheese

pepper, to taste

⅓ cup tomato salsa, to serve

⅓ cup sour cream, to serve

1. Put a large piece of double-thickness aluminum foil into the bottom of a nonstick skillet and put the skillet over medium–high heat.

2. Place the tortilla chips in a single layer on the foil. Sprinkle the chicken and cheese over the chips. Cover the skillet with either a lid or some foil.

3. Cook the nachos for about 10–15 minutes, until the cheese is just melting (check by opening up the foil regularly).

4. Season with pepper and serve the nachos with the salsa and sour cream liberally spooned over the top.

STICKY GINGER & SOY CHICKEN WINGS

It is always a particularly gratifying experience eating food with your fingers, and these sticky, sweet wings are a real treat.

SERVES: 4

PREP TIME: 15 MINS PLUS MARINATING

COOK TIME: 12–15 MINS

INGREDIENTS

12 chicken wings
2 garlic cloves, crushed
1-inch piece fresh ginger, peeled and chopped
2 tablespoons dark soy sauce
2 tablespoons lime juice
1 tablespoon honey
1 teaspoon chili sauce
2 teaspoons sesame oil
lime wedges, to serve

1. Tuck the pointed tip of each wing under the thicker end to make a neat triangle.

2. Mix together the garlic, ginger, soy sauce, lime juice, honey, chili sauce, and oil.

3. Spoon the mixture over the chicken and turn to coat evenly. Cover and marinate for several hours or overnight.

4. Preheat the broiler to hot and line the broiler pan with aluminum foil. Cook the wings on the prepared broiler pan for 12–15 minutes, or until the juices run clear when the tip of a sharp knife is inserted into the thickest part of the meat, basting often with the marinade.

5. Serve hot, with lime wedges.

HERO TIPS

If you are serving these delicious wings for guests, make sure that you have plenty of napkins and a finger bowl for cleaning sticky fingers.

2

3

4

CHICKEN WINGS

SERVES: 4

PREP TIME: 40–45 MINS   COOK TIME: 20–25 MINS

INGREDIENTS

12 chicken wings
1 egg
¼ cup milk
⅔ cup all-purpose flour
1 teaspoon paprika
2 cups dried bread crumbs
4 tablespoons butter
salt and pepper, to taste

1. Preheat the oven to 425°F. Separate each chicken wing into three pieces, discarding the bony tip. Beat the egg with the milk in a shallow dish.

2. Combine the flour and paprika in a shallow dish and season with salt and pepper. Place the bread crumbs in another dish. Dip the chicken in the egg mixture, drain, and roll in the flour.

3. Shake off any excess, then roll the chicken wings in the bread crumbs, gently pressing them onto the surface and shaking off any excess.

4. Put the butter in a wide, shallow roasting pan and place in the preheated oven to melt.

5. Place the chicken in the pan, skin-side down.

6. Bake for 10 minutes on each side. To check that the wings are cooked through, cut into the middle to check that there are no remaining traces of pink or red.

7. Transfer the chicken to a serving plate and serve.

BARBECUE-GLAZED DRUMSTICKS

SERVES: 6

PREP TIME: 15 MINS PLUS MARINATING

COOK TIME: 1 HR

INGREDIENTS

12 chicken drumsticks, about 3½ pounds in total

1 cup barbecue sauce

1 tablespoon packed light brown sugar

1 tablespoon cider vinegar

1 teaspoon salt

½ teaspoon pepper

½ teaspoon hot pepper sauce

vegetable oil, for brushing

salad, to serve

1. Using a sharp knife, make two slashes, about 1 inch apart, into the thickest part of the drumsticks, cutting to the bone. Put the drumsticks into a large, sealable plastic freezer bag.

2. Mix together ¼ cup of the barbecue sauce, the sugar, vinegar, salt, pepper, and hot pepper sauce in a small bowl. Pour the mixture into the bag, press out most of the air, and seal tightly. Shake the bag gently to distribute the sauce evenly and let marinate in the refrigerator for at least 4 hours.

3. Preheat the oven to 400°F. Line a baking sheet with aluminum foil and brush lightly with oil.

4. Using tongs, transfer the drumsticks to the prepared baking sheet. Discard the marinade. Brush both sides of the drumsticks with some of the remaining barbecue sauce.

5. Bake for 15 minutes, then remove from the oven and brush generously with more barbecue sauce. Return to the oven and repeat this process three more times for a total cooking time of 1 hour or until the chicken is tender and the juices run clear when the tip of a sharp knife is inserted into the thickest part of the meat. Serve with salad.

COUNT YOUR CHICKENS!

An average-size chicken weighs about 3¼ pounds and will feed a family of four with some leftovers for the next day. You can also make your own stock from the raw or cooked chicken carcass (see pages 50–51) to be used fresh (or frozen for later use) in recipes such as soups, risottos, casseroles, or stews. If you have a little extra time, it is usually much more economical to buy a whole chicken and separate the parts yourself than it is to buy chicken breast, thigh, and leg parts.

CUTTING UP A CHICKEN

When cutting up a chicken, it can be cut into either four parts (two legs and two breasts) or eight sections (two thighs, two drumsticks, two breasts, and two wings).

• Before cutting up the bird, remove and discard any trussing string. Using a large, sharp knife, remove and discard the wishbone. Using poultry shears or a sharp knife, pull out each wing, then cut off the wing tips (you can use the wing tips to make stock, along with the raw carcass).

• Position the chicken, breast-side up, on a cutting board, then cut down through the skin on one side of the chicken between the leg and the body, as close to the leg as possible. Bend the leg back (away from the body) as far as you can and twist sharply until you dislocate the ball-and-socket joint between the thigh bone and rib cage, then cut the leg away to release it from the body. Repeat the process with the other leg.

At this stage (if you want eight parts), each leg can be divided into thigh and drumstick. To do this, lay each leg part out on the cutting board, find the joint connecting the

24

drumstick to the thigh, and cut down through it to separate the leg into thigh and drumstick. Trim off the top end of the drumstick, too (these scraps can also be used to make stock). Repeat the process with the other leg.

• To remove each breast with the bone in, cut along one side of the length of the breastbone from neck to tail, using a sharp knife, then cut down as close to the bone as you can, following the contour of the breast meat. Using sharp kitchen scissors or poultry shears, cut through the rib bones that join the breast to the breastbone, then snip along the fat line on the other side of the breast (around the side of the breast), cutting through the meat and skin to remove the breast from the body. Trim away any unwanted flaps of skin or fat. Repeat the process on the other side.

At this stage (if you want eight parts), each breast can be cut diagonally in half, so one portion has a wing joint with some breast meat and the other one is just breast meat.

• To remove each breast from the bone, using a sharp knife, gently cut and ease the flesh away from the ribs, cutting down between the flesh and ribs of one breast and separating the meat from the ribs, following the shape of the rib cage/ breastbone underneath the meat. Cut the meat away neatly. Repeat the process on the other breast.

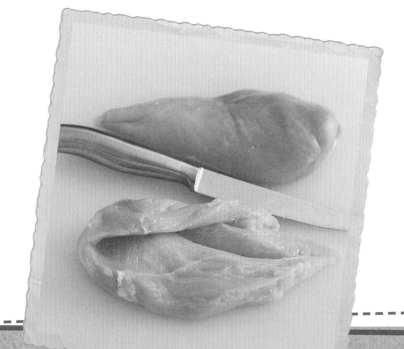

CHICKEN-LOADED POTATO SKINS

SERVES: 4 **PREP TIME: 15 MINS** **COOK TIME: 15–20 MINS**

INGREDIENTS

4 baking potatoes,
halved lengthwise

2 tablespoons sunflower oil,
plus extra for oiling

1 onion, finely chopped

2 tablespoons all-purpose flour

freshly grated nutmeg, to taste

1¼ cups milk

1½ cups diced, cooked
boneless, skinless chicken

1½ cups diced, cooked ham

2 sun-dried tomatoes in oil,
drained and thinly sliced

2 tablespoons chopped fresh
flat-leaf parsley, plus extra
to garnish

1 cup grated mozzarella cheese

salt and pepper, to taste

1. Preheat the broiler to high and position a rack 5 inches from the heat.

2. Scoop out the potato flesh, leaving a ¼-inch shell. (The flesh can be used in other recipes.) Rub the potato skins with oil, then season with salt and pepper.

3. Place the skins on a baking sheet, cut-side up, place under the broiler, and cook for 5 minutes. Turn and cook for an additional 3–5 minutes, until crisp. Remove from the heat, but do not turn off the broiler.

4. Meanwhile, heat the oil in a saucepan. Add the onion and sauté for 2–3 minutes, until soft. Add the flour and nutmeg and stir for 2 minutes, then slowly stir in the milk. Bring to a boil, then reduce the heat and simmer for 2 minutes.

5. Stir in the chicken, ham, tomatoes, and parsley and season with salt and pepper.

6. Divide the mixture among the potato skins and sprinkle with the cheese. Return to the broiler and cook for 4–5 minutes, or until the cheese is bubbling. Sprinkle with flat-leaf parsley and serve.

CHICKEN BALLS WITH DIPPING SAUCE

SERVES: 4   **PREP TIME: 20 MINS**   **COOK TIME: 10–15 MINS**

INGREDIENTS

2 large skinless, boneless chicken breasts
3 tablespoons vegetable oil
2 shallots, finely chopped
½ celery stalk, finely chopped
1 garlic clove, crushed
2 tablespoons light soy sauce
1 medium egg, lightly beaten
1 bunch of scallions
salt and pepper, to taste

DIPPING SAUCE

3 tablespoons dark soy sauce
1 tablespoon rice wine
1 teaspoon sesame seeds

1. Cut the chicken into ¾-inch pieces. Heat half of the oil in a skillet and stir-fry the chicken over high heat for 2–3 minutes, until golden. Remove from the skillet with a slotted spoon and set aside.

2. Add the shallots, celery, and garlic to the skillet and stir-fry for 1–2 minutes, until softened.

3. Place the chicken and the shallot mixture in a food processor and process until finely minced. Add 1 tablespoon of the light soy sauce and just enough of the egg to make a fairly firm mixture. Season with salt and pepper.

4. To make the dipping sauce, mix together the dark soy sauce, rice wine, and sesame seeds in a small serving bowl and set aside.

5. Shape the chicken mixture into 16 walnut-size balls. Heat the remaining oil in the skillet and stir-fry the chicken balls in small batches for 4–5 minutes, until golden brown. Drain on paper towels.

6. Add the scallions to the skillet and stir-fry for 1–2 minutes, until they begin to soften, then stir in the remaining light soy sauce. Serve the chicken balls with the stir-fried scallions and dipping sauce.

CHICKEN SATAY SKEWERS

SERVES: 4

PREP TIME: 15 MINS PLUS SOAKING & MARINATING

COOK TIME: 10 MINS

INGREDIENTS

4 skinless, boneless chicken breasts, about 4 ounces each, cut into ¾-inch cubes

¼ cup soy sauce

1 tablespoon cornstarch

2 garlic cloves, finely chopped

1-inch piece fresh ginger, peeled and finely chopped

1 cucumber, diced, to serve

PEANUT SAUCE

2 tablespoons peanut oil or vegetable oil

½ onion, finely chopped

1 garlic clove, finely chopped

¼ cup chunky peanut butter

¼ –⅓ cup water

½ teaspoon chili powder

1. Put the chicken cubes in a shallow dish. Mix together the soy sauce, cornstarch, garlic, and ginger in a small bowl and pour the marinade over the chicken. Cover and let marinate in the refrigerator for at least 2 hours.

2. Meanwhile, soak 12 wooden skewers in cold water for at least 30 minutes. Preheat the broiler and thread the chicken pieces onto the skewers. Transfer the skewers to a broiler pan and cook under the preheated broiler for 3–4 minutes. Turn the skewers over and cook for an additional 3–4 minutes or until cooked through. To check the chicken cubes are cooked through, cut into the middle to check that there are no remaining traces of pink or red.

3. Meanwhile, to make the sauce, heat the oil in a saucepan, add the onion and garlic, and cook over medium heat, stirring frequently, for 3–4 minutes, until softened. Add the peanut butter, water, and chili powder and simmer for 2–3 minutes, until softened and thinned. Serve the skewers immediately with the warm sauce and cucumber.

SAUTÉED CHICKEN & GARLIC

This is a gorgeous dish and works particularly well with some fresh crusty bread to help mop up all of the delicious juices.

SERVES: 8   **PREP TIME: 10 MINS**   **COOK TIME: 25–30 MINS**

INGREDIENTS

8 skin-on chicken thighs, boned if available

hot or sweet smoked paprika, to taste

¼ cup olive oil

10 garlic cloves, sliced

½ cup dry white wine

1 bay leaf

salt

fresh flat-leaf parsley, chopped, to garnish

crusty bread, to serve (optional)

1. If necessary, halve the chicken thighs and remove the bones, then cut the flesh into bite-size pieces, leaving the skin on. Season with paprika.

2. Heat the oil in a large skillet or Dutch oven, add the garlic slices, and cook over medium heat, stirring frequently, for 1 minute, until golden brown. Remove with a slotted spoon and drain on paper towels.

3. Add the chicken pieces to the skillet and cook, turning occasionally, for 10 minutes, or until tender and golden brown on all sides. Add the wine and bay leaf and bring to a boil. Reduce the heat and simmer, stirring occasionally, for 10 minutes, or until most of the liquid has evaporated and the juices run clear when the tip of a sharp knife is inserted into the thickest part of the meat. Remove and discard the bay leaf. Season with salt.

4. Transfer the chicken to a warmed serving dish and sprinkle with the reserved garlic slices. Sprinkle with chopped parsley to garnish and serve with chunks of crusty bread to mop up the juices, if desired.

CHICKEN ROLLS WITH OLIVES

These rolls look impressive but use few ingredients and take little time to prepare and cook. Serve to friends at a dinner party to create a real "wow" factor.

SERVES: 6–8　　　**PREP TIME: 15–20 MINS**　　**COOK TIME: 25–30 MINS**

INGREDIENTS

1 cup black ripe olives in oil, drained and 2 tablespoons oil reserved

1¼ sticks butter, softened

¼ cup chopped fresh parsley

4 skinless, boneless chicken breasts

1. Preheat the oven to 400°F. Pit and finely chop the olives. Mix together the olives, butter, and parsley in a bowl. Place the chicken breasts between two sheets of plastic wrap and gently beat with a meat mallet or the side of a rolling pin.

2. Spread the olive-and-parsley butter over one side of each flattened chicken breast and roll up.

3. Secure with wooden toothpicks or tie with kitchen string.

4. Place the chicken rolls in an ovenproof dish. Drizzle with the reserved oil from the olives and bake in the preheated oven for 25–30 minutes. Cut into the middle of the chicken to check there are no remaining traces of pink or red.

5. Transfer the chicken rolls to a cutting board, discard the toothpicks or string and slice with a sharp knife.

6. Transfer to a warmed serving plate and serve immediately.

CHICKEN PÂTÉ

SERVES: 4

**PREP TIME: 20–25 MINS   COOK TIME: 10–15 MINS
PLUS CHILLING**

INGREDIENTS

1¼ sticks butter
1 onion, finely chopped
1 garlic clove, finely chopped
8 ounces chicken livers
½ teaspoon Dijon mustard
2 tablespoons brandy (optional)
salt and pepper
whole-wheat toast strips and
green olives, to serve

CLARIFIED BUTTER

1 stick salted butter

1. Melt half the butter in a large skillet over medium heat and cook the onion for 3–4 minutes, until soft and transparent. Add the garlic and continue to cook for an additional 2 minutes.

2. Check the chicken livers and remove any discolored parts using a pair of scissors. Add the livers to the skillet and cook over high heat for 5–6 minutes, until browned.

3. Season well with salt and pepper and add the mustard and brandy, if using.

4. Process the pâté in a blender or food processor until smooth. Cut the remaining butter into small pieces, add to the blender, and process until creamy.

5. Press the pâté into a serving dish or four small ramekins (individual ceramic dishes), smooth over the surface, and cover with plastic wrap. If the pâté is to be kept for more than two days, cover the surface with a little clarified butter. In a clean saucepan, heat the butter until it melts, then continue heating for a few moments until it stops simmering. Let the sediment settle and carefully pour the clarified butter over the pâté.

6. Chill in the refrigerator until ready to serve, accompanied by toast strips and green olives.

PARMESAN CHICKEN TENDERS

The great things about these tender baked, cheesy chicken strips is that they are as popular with adults as with children, and they are equally good eaten hot or cold.

SERVES: 4

PREP TIME: 20 MINS PLUS MARINATING

COOK TIME: 20–25 MINS

INGREDIENTS

4 boneless, skinless chicken breasts, about 6 ounces each, cut across the grain into ½-inch-wide strips

⅔ cup panko bread crumbs, finely crushed

⅔ cup freshly grated Parmesan cheese

3 tablespoons all-purpose flour

¼ teaspoon baking powder

¼ teaspoon paprika, or to taste

olive oil or vegetable oil spray

cooked green vegetables, to serve

MARINADE

⅓ cup buttermilk

1 egg, lightly beaten

salt and pepper, to taste

1. To make the marinade, combine the buttermilk and egg in a large bowl and season with salt and pepper. Stir in the chicken strips, then cover the bowl and marinate in the refrigerator for 2–4 hours.

2. When ready to cook, preheat the oven to 375°F and line two baking sheets with parchment paper. Toss together the bread crumbs, cheese, flour, baking powder, and paprika in a wide bowl.

3. Remove a piece of chicken from the marinade, letting the excess drip back into the bowl. Place in the bread crumb mixture and toss until coated, then transfer to the prepared baking sheet. Continue until all the chicken pieces are coated. Lightly oil each piece.

4. Bake in the preheated oven for 20–25 minutes until golden brown. Cut into the middle of the chicken to check there are no remaining traces of pink or red. Serve with vegetables.

LOVELY LUNCHES

CHICKEN CAESAR SALAD

SERVES: 4 **PREP TIME: 20 MINS** **COOK TIME: 20 MINS**

INGREDIENTS

3 tablespoons sunflower oil

2 thick slices of white bread, cubed

2 skinless, boneless chicken breasts, about 5 ounces each

2 small heads of romaine lettuce, coarsely chopped

2 tablespoons Parmesan cheese shavings

salt and pepper, to taste

DRESSING

1 garlic clove, crushed

2 canned anchovy fillets, drained and finely chopped

$\frac{1}{3}$ cup light olive oil

2 tablespoons white wine vinegar

2 tablespoons mayonnaise

2 tablespoons freshly grated Parmesan cheese

salt and pepper, to taste

1. Preheat the oven to 400°F. Place 2 tablespoons of the sunflower oil in a bowl, add the bread, and toss to coat in the oil. Spread out on a baking sheet, season well with salt and pepper, and bake in the preheated oven for 10 minutes, until crisp and golden brown.

2. Meanwhile, brush the chicken breasts with the remaining sunflower oil and season with salt and pepper. Cook in a preheated cast-iron skillet for 8–10 minutes on each side, until the chicken is tender and the juices run clear when the tip of a sharp knife is inserted into the thickest part of the meat.

3. To make the dressing, place all the ingredients in a small bowl and mix thoroughly until smooth and creamy.

4. Slice the hot cooked chicken and toss lightly with the lettuce and croutons. Divide the salad among four serving bowls and drizzle with the dressing. Sprinkle the Parmesan cheese shavings over the top and serve immediately.

CHICKEN & PESTO SALAD

SERVES: 4

**PREP TIME: 15 MINS
PLUS COOLING &
CHILLING**

COOK TIME: 20–25 MINS

INGREDIENTS

4 large chicken thighs

sunflower oil or olive oil,
for brushing

8 ounces dried fusilli
(corkscrew pasta)

2 cups chopped green beans

1 cup prepared pesto,
plus extra if needed

2 large tomatoes, sliced

salt and pepper, to taste

fresh basil leaves, to garnish

1. Preheat the broiler to medium–high and position the broiler rack about 3 inches below the heat. Brush the chicken thighs with oil and season with salt and pepper. Brush the rack with a little oil, add the chicken thighs, skin-side up, and cook for 20–25 minutes, or until the chicken is cooked through and the juices run clear when the tip of a sharp knife is inserted into the thickest part of the meat. Remove from the heat and set aside.

2. Meanwhile, bring a large saucepan of lightly salted water to a boil. Add the pasta, return to a boil and cook for 8–10 minutes, or according to the package directions, until tender but still firm to the bite. Add the beans 5 minutes before the end of the cooking time.

3. Drain the pasta and beans, shaking off the excess water, and immediately transfer to a large bowl. Add the pesto and stir until the pasta and beans are well coated. Set aside to cool.

HERO TIPS

This is a perfect salad for a summer gathering. Try adding sun-dried tomatoes for a sweeter taste, or drizzle with balsamic vinegar to sharpen the flavors.

4. When the chicken is cool enough to handle, remove the skin and bones and cut the flesh into bite-size pieces. Stir into the pesto mixture and season with salt and pepper. Set aside to cool completely, then cover and chill until required. (It will keep for up to one day, covered, in the refrigerator.)

5. Remove the salad from the refrigerator 10 minutes before serving. Arrange the tomato slices on a serving plate. Stir the salad and add extra pesto, if needed. Mound the salad on top of the tomatoes, garnish with basil leaves, and serve immediately.

CREAM OF CHICKEN SOUP

SERVES: 4

PREP TIME: 15 MINS PLUS COOLING

COOK TIME: 40 MINS

INGREDIENTS

3 tablespoons butter

4 shallots, chopped

1 leek, sliced

1 pound skinless, boneless chicken breasts, chopped

2½ cups chicken stock

1 tablespoon chopped fresh parsley

1 tablespoon chopped fresh thyme, plus extra sprigs to garnish

¾ cup heavy cream

salt and pepper, to taste

1. Melt the butter in a large saucepan over medium heat. Add the shallots and cook, stirring, for 3 minutes, until slightly softened.

2. Add the leek and cook for an additional 5 minutes, stirring.

3. Add the chicken, stock, and herbs, and season with salt and pepper. Bring to a boil, then reduce the heat and simmer for 25 minutes, until the chicken is tender and cooked through. To check the chicken pieces are cooked through, cut into the middle to check that there are no remaining traces of pink or red.

4. Remove from the heat and let cool for 10 minutes. Transfer the soup to a food processor or blender and process until smooth (you may need to do this in batches).

5. Return the soup to the rinsed-out pan and warm over low heat for 5 minutes.

6. Stir in the cream and cook for an additional 2 minutes, then remove from the heat and ladle into warmed serving bowls. Garnish with thyme sprigs and serve immediately.

2

3

6

47

SPICY CHICKEN NOODLE SOUP

This quick, healthy, wholesome soup is a real winner for an instant meal that's packed with goodness. The main flavor comes from miso, a highly nutritious fermented paste used as the basis of many noodle soups.

SERVES: 2 **PREP TIME: 15 MINS** **COOK TIME: 5–10 MINS**

INGREDIENTS

1¼ cups chicken stock

1 cup boiling water

1 teaspoon miso paste

¾-inch piece fresh ginger, peeled and finely grated

1 red chile, seeded and thinly sliced

1 carrot, peeled and cut into thin strips

3 cups shredded bok choy

6 ounces dried cellophane noodles, cooked

1 cooked chicken breast, shredded

dark soy sauce, to taste

4 scallions, finely chopped

handful fresh cilantro, coarsely chopped, to serve

1. Place the stock and boiling water in a saucepan and bring to a boil over medium–high heat. Add the miso paste and simmer for 1–2 minutes.

2. Add the ginger, chile, carrot, bok choy, cooked noodles, and chicken. Simmer for an additional 4–5 minutes. Season with soy sauce.

3. Sprinkle the scallions in the bottom of two warmed serving bowls and pour the soup over them. Top with chopped cilantro and serve immediately.

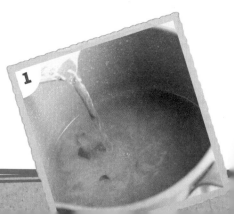

TAKE STOCK!

A good homemade stock will make a real difference to the overall flavor of many dishes, including soups, sauces, casseroles, and stews, so it is worth the effort to make your own. Homemade stock also freezes well, so it's a good idea to make a large batch and then cool and freeze it for future use.

CHICKEN STOCK

You can make two types of chicken stock: a light stock made from raw carcasses, and a brown stock made from a cooked carcass. It is more usual to prepare the latter (see recipe below), because we often have a carcass leftover from a roasted chicken, while it is less usual to have a whole fresh carcass.

Makes about 4 cups

1 carcass from a roasted chicken
6 cups water
1 onion, peeled and sliced
1 carrot, peeled and sliced
1 celery stalk, sliced
1 teaspoon dried thyme
1 bay leaf
3 sprigs fresh parsley
salt and pepper, to taste

1. Break up the chicken carcass and place it in a large (lidded) saucepan (about 3-quart capacity). Add the water, vegetables, and herbs. Season with salt and pepper and bring to a boil over medium heat. Skim the surface if any foam forms.

2. Cover the pan with the lid, lower the heat, and simmer for 1½–2 hours.

3. Remove from the heat, let cool a little, then strain through a strainer into a large bowl. Discard the contents of the strainer (including all the bones and any parts of meat, the vegetables, and herbs).

4. Cool completely, then remove all traces of fat from the top of the stock using a slotted spoon. If required, you can boil the stock (uncovered) for up to 30 minutes to reduce the stock and give a more intense flavor. Cover the cool stock with plastic wrap, store in the refrigerator, and use within two days.

Hero Tips

This stock is suitable for freezing. Chill thoroughly, then pour into a rigid, airtight (lidded) container, and freeze for up to three months. To use, thaw at room temperature or in the refrigerator and use as instructed.

OTHER STOCK PRODUCTS

If you are not able to make your own chicken stock, there is a good range of chicken stock and chicken broth products available to buy. These include bouillon cubes, granules, powder, concentrated liquid stock, chilled fresh stock or broth, as well as some reduced-sodium versions.

CHICKEN, MUSHROOM & HERB OMELET

Part of the versatility of chicken is that any leftovers are just as good as when cooked fresh. Omelets are the ultimate fast food. If making more than one, make them one after another and keep warm in an oven preheated to 300°F until they are all ready to serve.

MAKES: 1　　　　**PREP TIME: 10–15 MINS**　　**COOK TIME: 12 MINS**

INGREDIENTS

1 tablespoon butter

2 tablespoons sunflower oil

1½ cups sliced cremini mushrooms

½ cup thinly sliced, cooked boneless, skinless chicken

1 tablespoon chopped mixed fresh herbs, such as chervil, chives, parsley, and thyme, plus extra parsley to garnish

2 eggs

1 tablespoon milk or water

salt and pepper, to taste

1. Melt the butter with half the oil in an 8-inch skillet over medium–high heat. Add the mushrooms, season with salt and pepper, and sauté, stirring, for 5–8 minutes, until the mushrooms reabsorb the liquid they release.

2. Add the chicken and herbs and continue cooking to heat the chicken. Adjust the seasoning, if necessary. Remove from the skillet and keep hot.

3. Add the remaining oil to the skillet, heat until hot, and swirl around the bottom and side. Beat the eggs with the milk and season with salt and pepper.

4. When the oil is hot, pour the eggs into the skillet, tilting and rotating the pan so they cover the bottom evenly. Reduce the heat to low–medium.

5. Cook for 5–10 seconds, or until the omelet is set on the bottom. Spoon the chicken mixture into the center, then use a spatula to ease half the omelet over the filling. Slide the omelet out of the pan, garnish with parsley, and serve immediately.

53

SMOKED CHICKEN & HAM FOCACCIA

SERVES: 2–4   **PREP TIME: 15 MINS**   **COOK TIME: 5 MINS**

INGREDIENTS

1 thick focaccia loaf

handful of fresh basil leaves

2 small zucchini,
coarsely grated

6 wafer-thin slices of
smoked chicken

6 wafer-thin slices of
cooked ham

8 ounces Taleggio cheese,
cut into strips

freshly grated nutmeg
(optional)

cherry tomatoes and
salad greens, to serve

1. Preheat a broiler pan under the broiler until both broiler and pan are hot. Slice the focaccia in half horizontally and cut the top half lengthwise into strips.

2. Cover the bottom half of the focaccia with basil leaves, top with the zucchini in an even layer, and cover with the chicken and ham. Lay the strips of focaccia on top, placing strips of cheese between them. Sprinkle with a little nutmeg, if using.

3. Place the assembled bread on the hot pan and cook under the preheated broiler, well away from the heat, for about 5 minutes, until the cheese has melted and the top of the bread is browned. Cut the focaccia into four pieces and serve immediately with cherry tomatoes and salad greens.

CHICKEN & LIME TACOS

MAKES: 12

PREP TIME: 15 MINS PLUS MARINATING

COOK TIME: 20 MINS

INGREDIENTS

4 boneless, skinless chicken thighs

2 tablespoons freshly squeezed lime juice

1 tablespoon sunflower oil, plus extra for oiling

1 teaspoon ancho chili powder or paprika, or to taste

1 teaspoon ground cumin

1 teaspoon ground coriander

salt and pepper, to taste

CILANTRO & LIME RICE

1 cup instant long-grain rice

finely grated zest of 1 lime

2 tablespoons finely chopped cilantro

TO SERVE

12 crisp corn taco shells, warmed according to the package directions

shredded lettuce

guacamole

tomato salsa

sharp cheddar cheese or American cheese, finely grated

1. Put the chicken thighs into a nonmetallic dish and rub all over with the lime juice. Mix together the oil, chili powder, cumin, and ground coriander and season with salt and pepper. Rub all over the chicken thighs, then set them aside to marinate for 2 hours.

2. Meanwhile, cook the rice according to the package directions. Drain well and transfer to a bowl. Stir in the lime zest, cover, and keep warm while you cook the chicken.

3. Heat a ridged, cast-iron grill pan over high heat. Brush the ridges with oil and reduce the heat to medium. Add the chicken thighs and cook for 4 minutes, brushing once with any leftover marinade. Turn and cook for another 4 minutes, or until the chicken is cooked through and the juices run clear when the tip of a sharp knife is inserted into the thickest part of the meat. Slice into strips.

4. Stir the cilantro into the rice and adjust the seasoning, if necessary.

5. To assemble, divide the rice among the taco shells, then add the chicken. Top with lettuce, then add any of the suggested serving accompaniments. Serve immediately.

CHICKEN BURRITO BOWLS

SERVES: 4   **PREP TIME: 10 MINS**   **COOK TIME: 1¼ HRS**

INGREDIENTS

6 skinless chicken thighs on the bone

4 cups water

1 (14½-ounce) can diced tomatoes

2 bay leaves

2 pickled Serrano or jalapeño chiles, chopped

2 limes, sliced

1 onion, halved

1 tablespoon Mexican oregano

2 teaspoons ancho chili powder

2 teaspoons ground coriander

2 teaspoons ground cumin

1½ cups instant long-grain rice

salt and pepper, to taste

TO SERVE

chopped fresh cilantro

2 avocados, peeled, pitted, diced, and tossed with lime juice

other accompaniments of your choice, such as shredded cheeses, pitted black ripe olives, sour cream, and chopped jalapeño peppers

1. Put the chicken and water into a saucepan and slowly bring to a boil, skimming the surface as necessary. When the foam stops rising, stir in the tomatoes, bay leaves, chiles, lime slices, onion, oregano, chili powder, ground coriander, and cumin and season with salt and pepper. Adjust the heat so the liquid just bubbles, then let simmer for about 60 minutes, until the liquid evaporates and the meat is tender. The juices should run clear when the tip of a sharp knife is inserted into the thickest part of the meat.

2. Meanwhile, cook the rice according to the package directions, then drain well and keep hot.

3. Use a slotted spoon to transfer the chicken to a bowl. Remove the bones and use two forks to shred the meat. Adjust the seasoning, if necessary.

4. To serve, divide the rice among four warmed bowls, then top with the shredded chicken. Sprinkle with chopped cilantro and serve with the remaining accompaniments at the table.

CHICKEN FAJITAS

SERVES: 4

PREP TIME: 15 MINS PLUS MARINATING

COOK TIME: 12–15 MINS

INGREDIENTS

3 tablespoons olive oil, plus extra for drizzling

3 tablespoons maple syrup or honey

1 tablespoon red wine vinegar

2 garlic cloves, crushed

2 teaspoons dried oregano

1–2 teaspoons crushed red pepper flakes

4 skinless, boneless chicken breasts

2 red bell peppers, seeded and cut into 1-inch strips

salt and pepper, to taste

warmed flour tortillas and shredded lettuce, to serve

1. Put the oil, maple syrup, vinegar, garlic, oregano, and red pepper flakes into a large, shallow dish, season with salt and pepper, and mix together.

2. Slice the chicken across the grain into slices 1 inch thick. Toss in the marinade to coat. Cover and chill for 2–3 hours, turning occasionally.

3. Drain the chicken. Heat a ridged grill pan until hot. Add the chicken and cook over medium–high heat for 3–4 minutes on each side. To check that the meat is cooked through, cut into the middle to check that there are no remaining traces of pink or red. Transfer to a warmed plate.

4. Add the bell peppers, skin-side down, to the pan and cook for 2 minutes on each side, until cooked through. Transfer to the plate with the chicken.

5. Divide the chicken and bell peppers among the flour tortillas, top with a little shredded lettuce, wrap, and serve immediately.

CAJUN CHICKEN

SERVES: 2   **PREP TIME: 10 MINS**   **COOK TIME: 25-30 MINS**

INGREDIENTS

4 chicken drumsticks
4 chicken thighs
2 ears of fresh corn, shucked
6 tablespoons butter, melted
oil, for frying

SPICE MIX

2 teaspoons onion powder
2 teaspoons paprika
1½ teaspoons salt
1 teaspoon garlic powder
1 teaspoon dried thyme
1 teaspoon cayenne pepper
1 teaspoon ground
black pepper
½ teaspoon ground
white pepper
¼ teaspoon ground cumin

1. Using a sharp knife, make two to three diagonal slashes in the chicken drumsticks and thighs, then place them in a large dish. Add the ears of corn.

2. Mix all the ingredients for the spice mix together in a small bowl. Brush the chicken and corn with the melted butter and sprinkle with the spice mix. Toss to coat well.

3. Heat the oil in a large ridged grill pan over medium–high heat and cook the chicken, turning occasionally, for 15 minutes, then add the ears of corn and cook, turning occasionally, for another 10–15 minutes, or until beginning to blacken slightly at the edges. Check the chicken is tender and the juices run clear when the tip of a sharp knife is inserted into the thickest part of the meat. Transfer to a serving plate and serve.

HERO TIPS

This summery dish is also delicious made on the barbecue. Simply place onto a preheated and lightly oiled grill rack and cook as instructed above.

CHICKEN & CASHEW NUTS

SERVES: 6

PREP TIME: 20 MINS PLUS MARINATING AND SOAKING

COOK TIME: 10–15 MINS

INGREDIENTS

1 pound boneless, skinless chicken breast

3 dried Chinese mushrooms, soaked in warm water for 20 minutes

2 tablespoons vegetable oil or peanut oil

4 slices fresh ginger

1 teaspoon minced garlic

1 red bell pepper, seeded and cut into 1-inch squares

1 tablespoon light soy sauce

¾ cup cashew nuts, toasted

MARINADE

2 tablespoons light soy sauce

1 teaspoon Chinese rice wine

pinch of sugar

1. Cut the chicken into cubes and put in a dish. Combine the marinade ingredients and pour over the chicken. Let marinate for at least 20 minutes.

2. Squeeze any excess water from the mushrooms and finely slice, discarding any tough stems. Reserve the soaking water.

3. Heat a wok over high heat, then add 1 tablespoon of oil. Add the ginger and stir-fry until fragrant. Stir in the chicken and cook for 2 minutes, until it turns golden brown. Before the chicken is cooked through, remove and set aside.

4. Wipe out the wok with paper towels. Heat the wok over high heat and add the remaining oil. Add the garlic and cook, stirring, for 1 minute. Add the mushrooms and red bell pepper and stir-fry for an additional 2 minutes. Add about 2 tablespoons of the mushroom soaking water and cook for about 2 minutes, or until the water has evaporated.

5. Return the chicken to the wok, add the soy sauce and the cashew nuts and stir-fry for 2 minutes. Cut into the middle of the chicken to check there are no remaining traces of pink or red. Serve immediately.

JERK CHICKEN BURGERS

MAKES: 4   PREP TIME: 25 MINS   COOK TIME: 20–25 MINS

INGREDIENTS

1 teaspoon packed light brown sugar
1 teaspoon ground ginger
½ teaspoon ground allspice
½ teaspoon dried thyme
½–1 teaspoon cayenne pepper or chopped fresh jalapeño chile
1 tablespoon lime juice
2 garlic cloves, finely chopped
½ teaspoon salt
½ teaspoon pepper
1 pound ground chicken
1 tablespoon vegetable oil
1 red bell pepper or yellow bell pepper, seeded and cut into large flat pieces
1 teaspoon olive oil
1 teaspoon red wine vinegar
4 onion rolls, halved
lettuce leaves
salt and pepper, to taste

1. Put the sugar, ginger, allspice, thyme, cayenne pepper, lime juice, garlic, salt, and pepper into a bowl and mix together. Add the chicken and gently mix to combine. Divide the mixture into four equal-size portions and shape each portion into a patty.

2. Place a ridged grill pan over medium–high heat and add the vegetable oil. Add the red bell pepper and cook for about 5 minutes, turning frequently, until blackened. Transfer to a bowl, cover with plastic wrap or a plate, and let steam for 5 minutes. Remove the skin and cut the flesh into strips. Toss with the olive oil, vinegar, and season with salt and pepper.

3. Put the patties in the pan and cook, covered, for about 5 minutes on each side, until brown and cooked through. Place the burgers in the rolls and top with the lettuce and bell peppers. Serve immediately.

 HERO TIPS

To spice up these burgers even more, serve with whole pickled jalapeños on the side, or use them chopped to top your burger.

PESTO CHICKEN PIZZA

Leftover chicken and store-bought pizza crusts make for the perfect quick-and-easy dinner. You can vary the toppings according to taste, but this recipe is always a winner.

MAKES: TWO 10½-INCH PIZZAS   **PREP TIME:** 10 MINS   **COOK TIME:** 10–12 MINS

INGREDIENTS

two 10½-inch store-bought pizza crusts

½–⅔ cup store-bought pesto

1¼ cups cooked chicken strips

⅓ cup drained, canned corn kernels

6 cherry tomatoes, thinly sliced

8 ounces mozzarella cheese, drained and coarsely torn

salt and pepper, to taste

1. Preheat the oven to 425°F. Put the pizza crusts on two baking sheets.

2. Divide the pesto between the two pizza crusts, spreading almost to the edges. Sprinkle with the chicken, corn, and tomatoes. Top with the cheese and season with salt and pepper.

3. Bake in the preheated oven for 10–12 minutes, or until the cheese is melting and turning golden and the crusts are crisp underneath. Serve immediately.

CHICKEN DINNERS

ROASTED CHICKEN

SERVES: 6 **PREP TIME: 15 MINS** **COOK TIME: 2 HRS 10 MINS PLUS RESTING**

INGREDIENTS

1 (5-pound) chicken

4 tablespoons butter, softened

2 tablespoons chopped fresh lemon thyme, plus extra sprigs to garnish

1 lemon, cut into quarters

½ cup white wine, plus extra if needed

salt and pepper, to taste

1. Preheat the oven to 425°F. Put the chicken into a roasting pan. Put the butter and thyme in a bowl, season with salt and pepper, mix together, and use to butter the chicken.

2. Place the lemon inside the cavity. Pour the wine over the chicken and roast in the preheated oven for 15 minutes. Reduce the temperature to 375°F and roast, basting frequently, for another 1¾ hours.

3. To check a whole bird is cooked through, a meat thermometer should read 180°F. Alternatively, pierce the thickest part of the leg between the drumstick and the thigh with the tip of a sharp knife. Any juices should be piping hot and clear with no traces of red or pink. To farther check, gently pull the leg away from the body, the leg should "give" and no traces of pinkness or blood should remain. Transfer to a warm plate, cover with aluminum foil, and let rest for 10 minutes.

4. Place the roasting pan on the stove and simmer the pan juices gently over low heat until they have reduced and are thick and glossy. Season and reserve.

5. To carve the chicken, place on a clean cutting board. Using a carving knife and fork, cut between the wings and the side of the breast. Remove the wings and cut slices off the breast.

6. Cut the legs from the body and cut through the joint to make drumsticks and thigh parts. Serve with the pan juices, garnished with thyme sprigs.

FRIED CHICKEN WITH TOMATO & BACON SAUCE

This wonderfully rich dish can be served with so many different sides. Try it with pasta or vegetables or even just some fresh bread to help mop up all of the delicious sauce.

SERVES: 4　　　**PREP TIME: 20 MINS**　　　**COOK TIME: 45 MINS**

INGREDIENTS

2 tablespoons butter

2 tablespoons olive oil

4 skinless, boneless chicken breasts or 8 skinless, boneless chicken thighs

TOMATO & BACON SAUCE

2 tablespoons butter

2 tablespoons olive oil

1 large onion, finely chopped

2 garlic cloves, finely chopped

1 celery stalk, finely chopped

4 bacon strips, diced

1 (14½-ounce) can diced tomatoes

2 tablespoons tomato paste

brown sugar, to taste

½ cup water

1 tablespoon chopped fresh basil

1 tablespoon chopped fresh flat-leaf parsley, plus extra to garnish

salt and pepper, to taste

1. First, make the tomato and bacon sauce. Melt the butter with the oil in a large saucepan. Add the onion, garlic, celery, and bacon and cook over low heat, stirring occasionally, for 5 minutes, until softened. Stir in the tomatoes, tomato paste, sugar, and water and season with salt and pepper. Increase the heat to medium and bring to a boil, then reduce the heat and simmer, stirring occasionally, for 15–20 minutes, until thickened.

2. Meanwhile, melt the butter with the oil in a large skillet. Add the chicken and cook over medium–high heat for 4–5 minutes on each side, until evenly browned.

3. Stir the basil and parsley into the sauce. Add the chicken and spoon the sauce over it. Cover and simmer for 10–15 minutes. Check the chicken is cooked through and the juices run clear when the tip of a sharp knife is inserted into the thickest part of the meat. Garnish with parsley and serve.

MOZZARELLA-STUFFED CHICKEN BREASTS

SERVES: 4   **PREP TIME: 15 MINS**   **COOK TIME: 15–20 MINS**

INGREDIENTS

4 skinless, boneless chicken breasts

4 teaspoons shop-bought green pesto

4 ounces mozzarella cheese

4 thin slices prosciutto

16 cherry tomatoes, halved

⅓ cup dry white wine or chicken stock

1 tablespoon olive oil

salt and pepper, to taste

fresh ciabatta, to serve

1. Preheat the oven to 425°F. Put the chicken breasts onto a cutting board and cut a deep pocket into each with a sharp knife.

2. Place a teaspoonful of pesto in each pocket.

3. Cut the cheese into four equal pieces and divide among the chicken breasts, tucking into the pockets.

4. Wrap a slice of prosciutto around each chicken breast to enclose the filling, with the seam underneath.

5. Place the chicken in a shallow ovenproof dish and arrange the tomatoes around it.

6. Season with salt and pepper, pour the wine over the chicken, and drizzle with the oil.

7. Bake in the preheated oven for 15–20 minutes, or until cooked through and the juices run clear when the tip of a sharp knife is inserted into the thickest part of the meat.

8. Cut the chicken breasts in half diagonally, place on warmed serving plates with the tomatoes, and spoon over the juices. Serve the chicken with ciabatta.

CHICKEN WITH CHILE & CILANTRO BUTTER

SERVES: 4   PREP TIME: 15 MINS   COOK TIME: 20 MINS

INGREDIENTS

4 tablespoons butter, softened

1 fresh Thai chile, seeded and chopped

3 tablespoons chopped fresh cilantro

4 skinless, boneless chicken breasts, about 6 ounces each

1¾ cups coconut milk

1½ cups chicken stock

1 cup long-grain rice

salt and pepper, to taste

PICKLED VEGETABLES

1 carrot

½ cucumber

3 scallions

2 tablespoons rice vinegar

1. Mix the butter with the chile and cilantro.

2. Cut a deep slash into the side of each chicken breast to form a pocket.

3. Spoon one-quarter of the butter into each pocket and place on a 12-inch square of parchment paper.

4. Season with salt and pepper, then bring together two opposite sides of the paper on top, folding over to seal firmly. Twist the ends to seal.

5. Pour the coconut milk and stock into a large saucepan with a steamer top. Bring to a boil. Stir in the rice with a pinch of salt.

6. Place the chicken packages in the steamer top, cover, and simmer for 15–18 minutes, stirring the rice once, until the rice is tender and the chicken juices run clear when the tip of a sharp knife is inserted into the thickest part of the meat.

7. Meanwhile, trim the carrot, cucumber, and scallions and cut into fine matchsticks. Sprinkle with the rice vinegar.

8. Unwrap the chicken, reserving the juices, and cut in half diagonally. Serve the chicken over the rice, with the juices spooned over and pickled vegetables on the side.

1

3

6

CHICKEN & RAMEN NOODLES

SERVES: 2　　　　　**PREP TIME: 15 MINS**　　　　　**COOK TIME: APPROX. 10 MINS**

INGREDIENTS

1 pound ramen noodles
1 onion, finely sliced
2 cups bean sprouts
1 red bell pepper, seeded and sliced
1 cup sliced, cooked chicken
12 cooked, peeled shrimp
1 tablespoon oil, for stir-frying
2 tablespoons Japanese soy sauce
1½ teaspoons mirin
1 teaspoon sesame oil
1 teaspoon sesame seeds
2 scallions, finely sliced

1. Cook the noodles according to the package directions, drain well, and transfer to a bowl.

2. Mix together the onion, bean sprouts, red bell pepper, chicken, and shrimp in a bowl. Stir through the noodles. Meanwhile, preheat a wok over high heat, add the oil, and heat until hot.

3. Add the noodle mixture and stir-fry for 4 minutes, or until golden, then add the soy sauce, mirin, and sesame oil and toss together.

4. Divide the noodles between two bowls.

5. Sprinkle with sesame seeds and scallions and serve.

HERO TIPS

To speed things up—and for any vegetarian guests—this recipe works equally well made with fresh vegetables and omitting the meat.

GREEN CHICKEN CURRY

This curry would be delicious with straight-to-wok noodles.
Stir them into the curry when the chicken is cooked.

SERVES: 4　　　　**PREP TIME: 10 MINS**　　　**COOK TIME: 15 MINS**

INGREDIENTS

2 tablespoons peanut oil
or vegetable oil
4 scallions, coarsely chopped
2 tablespoons green curry paste
3 cups coconut milk
1 chicken bouillon cube
6 skinless, boneless chicken
breasts, cut into 1-inch cubes
large handful of fresh
cilantro, chopped
½ teaspoon salt
cooked rice, to serve

1. Heat a wok over medium–high heat, then add the oil. Add the scallions and stir-fry for 30 seconds, or until starting to soften.

2. Add the curry paste, coconut milk, and bouillon cube and bring gently to a boil, stirring occasionally.

3. Add the chicken, half the cilantro, and the salt and stir well. Reduce the heat and simmer gently for 8–10 minutes, or until the chicken is cooked through. To check, cut into the middle of a chicken piece to check that there are no remaining traces of pink or red. Stir in the remaining cilantro. Serve immediately with freshly cooked rice.

CHICKEN FEED!

• Most whole fresh chickens sold in supermarkets and butchers are oven-ready and are often trussed (tied with string). Check the expiration date on the label and choose a plump bird (or chicken parts) with whitish pink or golden yellow skin (depending on the variety— for example, corn-fed chickens have a yellow hue to their skin and flesh) with no dry patches or signs of damage or blemishes.

• Store fresh chicken loosely covered (with plastic wrap or aluminum foil) in a shallow dish or container in the refrigerator for up to two days (or according to the expiration date on the label). If you buy a whole chicken that comes with giblets, remove the giblets and keep them in a separate covered container in the

refrigerator and use within one day (or discard the giblets if you are not going to be using them). Chicken livers and ground chicken should be used within 24 hours of purchase.

• Store raw chicken on a low shelf in the coldest part of your refrigerator to prevent any juices from dripping or leaking onto any foods below and to avoid the risk of cross contamination. Remember that raw and cooked chicken should always be stored separately.

• Freeze chicken on the day of purchase. Freeze fresh raw chicken for up to three months (and freeze cooked chicken for up to two months). Thaw frozen chicken in the refrigerator overnight (in a dish to catch any dripping juices) until it is completely thawed, and cook it as soon as possible and within 24 hours. Do not refreeze thawed chicken; however, you can freeze it again once it is cooked.

• It is essential to store, handle, and cook chicken correctly because raw or undercooked chicken may contain harmful bacteria, such as salmonella, that can cause food poisoning. Always wash your hands thoroughly before and after handling raw or cooked chicken, and make sure work surfaces and utensils are cleaned with hot soapy water. Disinfect worktops after use, preferably with a mild detergent or an antibacterial cleaner, and always use separate cutting boards and utensils when preparing raw and cooked chicken.

• Always make sure the chicken is thoroughly cooked before serving—it should be piping hot throughout, with no signs of pinkness when you cut into the thickest part of the meat. If you are roasting a whole bird, it is cooked when a meat thermometer inserted into the thickest part of the meat—in the inner thigh area near the breast—without touching the bone, has a reading of 180°F, or when you pierce the thigh with the tip of a sharp knife and the juices run clear. If the juices are pink or there are traces of blood, continue roasting the chicken until the juices run clear.

• Store leftover cooked chicken in a covered or airtight container in the refrigerator and use within one or two days. If you are reheating dishes containing chicken, make sure they are reheated thoroughly and are piping hot throughout before serving them.

INDIVIDUAL CHICKEN PIES

MAKES: 6

PREP TIME: 25 MINS

COOK TIME: 1 HR 20 MINS PLUS STANDING

INGREDIENTS

1 tablespoon olive oil

4 cups sliced button mushrooms

1 onion, finely chopped

6 carrots, sliced

2 celery stalks, sliced

4 cups cold chicken stock

6 tablespoons butter

⅓ cup all-purpose flour, plus extra for dusting

2 pounds skinless, boneless chicken breasts, cut into 1-inch cubes

¾ cup frozen peas

1 teaspoon chopped fresh thyme

1½ pounds ready-to-bake rolled dough pie crust, thawed if frozen

1 egg, lightly beaten

salt and pepper, to taste

1. Preheat the oven to 400°F. Heat the oil in a large saucepan. Add the mushrooms and onion and cook over medium heat, stirring frequently, for 8 minutes, until golden.

2. Add the carrots, celery, and half the stock and bring to a boil. Reduce the heat to low and simmer for 12–15 minutes, until the vegetables are almost tender.

3. Meanwhile, melt the butter in a large saucepan over medium heat. Whisk in the flour and cook, stirring constantly, for 4 minutes.

4. Gradually whisk in the remaining stock, then reduce the heat to low–medium and simmer, stirring, until thick. Stir in the vegetable mixture and add the chicken, peas, and thyme.

5. Simmer, stirring constantly, for 5 minutes. Taste and adjust the seasoning, adding salt and pepper, if needed. Divide the mixture among six large ramekins (individual ceramic dishes).

6. Roll out the dough on a floured surface and cut out six circles, each 1 inch larger than the diameter of the ramekins.

7. Place the dough circles on top of the filling, then crimp the edges. Cut a small cross in the center of each circle.

8. Put the ramekins on a baking sheet and brush the tops with beaten egg. Bake in the preheated oven for 35–40 minutes, until golden brown and bubbling. Let stand for 15 minutes before serving.

CHICKEN CASSEROLE

Like most casserole-style dishes, this recipe is equally good served the day it is cooked or up to a day later. If you are reheating, bring the vegetables to a boil, then return the chicken pieces to the pan and reduce the heat to avoid overcooking the chicken.

SERVES: 4 **PREP TIME: 10 MINS** **COOK TIME: 50 MINS**

INGREDIENTS

4 chicken legs, about 12 ounces each

2 tablespoons olive oil

2 red bell peppers, seeded and thickly sliced

1 large zucchini, halved lengthwise and thinly sliced

1 large onion, finely chopped

1 fennel bulb, thickly sliced lengthwise

1 (28-ounce) can diced tomatoes

1 tablespoon dried dill

1 tablespoon balsamic vinegar

pinch of light brown sugar

salt and pepper, to taste

fresh crusty bread, to serve

1. Preheat the oven to 375°F. Leave the chicken legs whole or cut them into drumsticks and thighs.

2. Heat the oil in a skillet. Add the chicken pieces, working in batches, if necessary, and cook for 5–7 minutes, until golden brown. Remove from the skillet and keep hot.

3. Pour off all but 2 tablespoons of the oil. Add the red bell peppers, zucchini, onion, and fennel and cook, stirring, for 3–5 minutes, until the onion is soft. Stir in the tomatoes, dill, vinegar, and sugar and season with salt and pepper.

4. Bring to a boil, stirring. Place the chicken pieces in a baking pan and pour the vegetables over the top. Cover tightly with aluminum foil, with the shiny side down.

5. Bake in the preheated oven for 30–35 minutes, until the chicken is cooked through and the juices run clear when the tip of a sharp knife is inserted into the thickest part of the meat. Serve with bread.

CHEDDAR & APPLE-STUFFED CHICKEN BREASTS

SERVES: 4   **PREP TIME: 15 MINS**   **COOK TIME: 25–30 MINS**
PLUS STANDING

INGREDIENTS

4 thick boneless, skinless
chicken breasts, about
7 ounces each

1 tablespoon sunflower oil, plus
extra for oiling

1 small onion, finely chopped

1 celery stalk, finely chopped

¼ teaspoon dried sage

1 Pippin or other crisp apple,
cored and diced

¾ cup cheddar, American, or
Muenster cheese

2 tablespoons finely chopped
parsley, plus extra to garnish

6 slices prosciutto

salt and pepper, to taste

cooked green vegetables,
to serve

1. Preheat the oven to 375°F and lightly oil a small roasting pan.

2. Put a chicken breast on a cutting board, rounded side up. Use a small, sharp knife to cut a pocket along the length of the breast, cutting as deep as you can without cutting through to the other side or the ends. Repeat with the remaining chicken breasts, then set aside.

3. To make the stuffing, heat the oil in a skillet, add the onion, celery, and sage, and sauté, stirring, for 3–5 minutes, until soft. Stir in the apple and sauté for an additional 2 minutes, until it is soft but not falling apart. Stir in the cheese and parsley and season with salt and pepper.

4. Divide the stuffing among the breast pockets. Wrap 1½ slices of prosciutto around each breast, then rub the tops with a little oil.

5. Transfer to the prepared pan and roast in the preheated oven for 20–25 minutes, or until the chicken is cooked through and the juices run clear when the tip of a sharp knife is inserted into the thickest part of the meat. Remove from the oven, cover with aluminum foil, and let stand for 3–5 minutes before serving with green vegetables.

SPICED CHICKEN STEW

SERVES: 6   **PREP TIME: 10 MINS**   **COOK TIME: APPROX. 1½ HRS**

INGREDIENTS

4 pounds chicken parts
2 tablespoons paprika
2 tablespoons olive oil
2 tablespoons butter
3 onions, chopped
2 yellow bell peppers, seeded and chopped
1 (14½-ounce) can diced tomatoes
1 cup dry white wine
2 cups chicken stock
1 tablespoon Worcestershire sauce
½ teaspoon Tabasco sauce
1 tablespoon finely chopped fresh flat-leaf parsley, plus extra to garnish
1 (11-ounce) can corn kernels, drained
1 (15-ounce) can lima beans, drained and rinsed
2 tablespoons all-purpose flour
¼ cup water
salt, to taste

1. Season the chicken pieces well with salt and dust with the paprika.

2. Heat the oil and butter in a Dutch oven or large saucepan. Add the chicken and cook over medium heat, turning, for 10–15 minutes, or until browned all over. Transfer to a plate with a slotted spoon.

3. Add the onions and bell peppers to the pan. Cook over low heat, stirring occasionally, for 5 minutes, or until softened. Add the tomatoes, wine, stock, Worcestershire sauce, Tabasco sauce, and parsley and bring to a boil, stirring. Return the chicken to the pan, cover, and simmer, stirring occasionally, for 30 minutes.

4. Add the corn and lima beans to the pan, partly replace the lid, and simmer for an additional 30 minutes, or until the chicken is tender and the juices run clear when the tip of a sharp knife is inserted into the thickest part of the meat.

5. Put the flour and water in a small bowl and mix to make a paste. Stir a ladleful of the cooking liquid into the paste, then stir the paste into the stew. Cook, stirring frequently, for an additional 5 minutes. Garnish with parsley and serve.

CHICKEN KIEV

This well-loved chicken classic is surprisingly easy to make. The garlic butter helps keep the chicken beautifully moist and the bread crumbs offer a delicious golden crunch.

MAKES: 8

PREP TIME: 15 MINS PLUS CHILLING

COOK TIME: APPROX. 30 MINS

INGREDIENTS

1 stick butter, softened

3–4 garlic cloves, minced

1 tablespoon chopped fresh parsley

1 tablespoon snipped fresh chives

juice and finely grated zest of ½ lemon

8 skinless, boneless chicken breasts, about 4 ounces each

⅓ cup all-purpose flour

2 eggs, lightly beaten

2 cups dried bread crumbs

peanut oil or sunflower oil, for deep-frying

salt and pepper, to taste

cooked green vegetables, to serve

1. Beat the butter in a bowl with the garlic, herbs, and lemon juice and zest. Season with salt and pepper. Divide into eight pieces, then shape into cylinders. Wrap in aluminum foil and chill in the refrigerator until firm.

2. Place each chicken breast between two sheets of plastic wrap. Pound gently with a meat mallet or rolling pin to flatten the chicken to an even thickness. Place a butter cylinder on each chicken piece and roll up. Secure with toothpicks.

3. Place the flour, eggs, and bread crumbs in separate shallow dishes. Dip the rolls into the flour, then the egg, and, finally, the bread crumbs. Chill in the refrigerator for 1 hour.

4. Heat enough oil for deep-frying in a saucepan or deep fryer to 350–375°F, or until a cube of bread browns in 30 seconds. Deep-fry the chicken, in batches, for 8–10 minutes, or until cooked through and golden brown. Drain on paper towels. Serve immediately with green vegetables.

CHICKEN BREASTS BRAISED WITH BABY VEGETABLES

The perfect thing about this dish is that it is all cooked in one pot, saving on both time and washing dishes. It serves as a great Sunday roast alternative.

SERVES: 4   **PREP TIME: 10 MINS**   **COOK TIME: 30 MINS**

INGREDIENTS

4 skinless chicken breasts
1 tablespoon butter
1 tablespoon olive oil
8 shallots
1 cup chicken stock
12 baby carrots
8 baby turnips
2 bay leaves
1 cup fresh or frozen peas
salt and pepper, to taste
boiled new potatoes, to serve

1. Cut deep slashes through the chicken at intervals and sprinkle with salt and pepper.

2. Heat the butter and oil in a wide saucepan or Dutch oven, add the chicken breasts and shallots, and cook, turning, for 3–4 minutes, until browned.

3. Add the stock and bring to a boil, then add the carrots, turnips, and bay leaves. Reduce the heat, cover, and simmer gently for 20 minutes.

4. Stir in the peas and cook for an additional 5 minutes. Check the chicken and vegetables are tender and the juices of the meat run clear when the tip of a sharp knife is inserted into the thickest part of the meat.

5. Adjust the seasoning to taste, remove and discard the bay leaves, and serve with new potatoes.

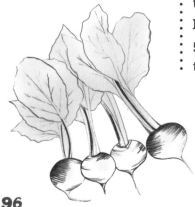

CREAMY CHICKEN PENNE

SERVES: 2   **PREP TIME: 5 MINS**   **COOK TIME: APPROX. 20 MINS**

INGREDIENTS

8 ounces dried penne
1 tablespoon olive oil
2 skinless, boneless chicken breasts
¼ cup dry white wine
¾ cup frozen peas
⅓ cup heavy cream
salt, to taste
¼ –⅓ cup chopped fresh flat-leaf parsley, to garnish

1. Bring a large saucepan of lightly salted water to a boil. Add the pasta, bring back to a boil, and cook for about 8–10 minutes, or according to the package directions, until tender but still firm to the bite.

2. Meanwhile, heat the oil in a skillet. Add the chicken and cook over medium heat for about 4 minutes on each side.

3. Pour in the wine and cook over high heat until it has almost evaporated.

4. Drain the pasta. Add the peas, cream, and pasta to the skillet and stir well. Cover and simmer for 2 minutes. Check the chicken is cooked through and the juices run clear when the tip of a sharp knife is inserted into the thickest part of the meat.

5. Garnish the chicken and pasta mixture with parsley and serve immediately.

HERO TIPS

For a healthier version, use light sour cream instead of the heavy cream. Or if you want to up the calorie intake, garnish with grated Parmesan cheese!

FOOD FOR FRIENDS

CHICKEN RISOTTO WITH SAFFRON

SERVES: 4   **PREP TIME: 5 MINS**   **COOK TIME: APPROX. 45 MINS**

INGREDIENTS

1 stick butter

2 pounds skinless, boneless chicken breasts, thinly sliced

1 large onion, chopped

2⅔ cups risotto rice

⅔ cup white wine

1 teaspoon crumbled saffron threads

5½ cups hot chicken stock

⅔ cup Parmesan cheese

salt and pepper, to taste

1. Heat 4 tablespoons of the butter in a deep saucepan. Add the chicken and onion and cook, stirring frequently, for 8 minutes, or until golden brown and cooked through. To check the chicken pieces are cooked through, cut into the middle to check that there are no remaining traces of pink or red.

2. Add the rice and mix to coat in the butter. Cook, stirring constantly, for 2–3 minutes, or until the grains are translucent.

3. Add the wine and cook, stirring constantly, for 1 minute, until reduced.

4. Mix the saffron with ¼ cup of the hot stock. Add the liquid to the rice and cook, stirring constantly, until it is absorbed.

5. Gradually add the remaining hot stock, a ladleful at a time. Add more liquid as the rice absorbs each addition. Cook, stirring, for 20 minutes, or until all the liquid is absorbed and the rice is creamy.

6. Remove from the heat and add the remaining butter. Mix well, then stir in the Parmesan cheese until it melts. Season with salt and pepper. Spoon the risotto into warmed serving dishes and serve immediately.

CHICKEN PARMESAN

SERVES: 4

PREP TIME: 15 MINS

COOK TIME: APPROX. 1 HR

INGREDIENTS

¾ cup all-purpose flour

2 eggs

2 cups dried bread crumbs

4 skinless, boneless chicken breasts, about 9 ounces each

2 tablespoons olive oil, plus extra if needed

8 ounces mozzarella, sliced

1½ cups grated Parmesan cheese

chopped fresh flat-leaf parsley, to garnish

SIMPLE MARINARA SAUCE

2 tablespoons olive oil

1 large onion, chopped

2 large garlic cloves, chopped

1 tablespoon dried mixed herbs

1 (28-ounce) can diced tomatoes

1 cup tomato puree or tomato sauce

2 teaspoon dried oregano

pinch of sugar

salt and pepper, to taste

1. To make the sauce, heat the oil in a large saucepan. Add the onion and sauté, stirring, for 2 minutes. Add the garlic and cook, stirring, until the onion is soft. Stir in the mixed herbs, tomatoes, tomato puree, oregano, and sugar and season with salt and pepper. Bring to a boil, then cover and simmer for 15 minutes. Transfer to a blender or food processor and puree.

2. Meanwhile, preheat the oven to 400°F. Spread the flour over a plate. Beat the eggs in a wide bowl, and put the bread crumbs on another plate. Halve the chicken breasts horizontally.

3. Place the chicken breasts between sheets of plastic wrap and pound with a meat mallet or rolling pin until about ¼ inch thick. Season both sides with salt and pepper. Dust a chicken breast with flour, shaking off the excess, then dip in the egg to coat. Dip in the bread crumbs to coat both sides, then set aside and repeat with the remaining chicken breasts.

4. Heat the oil in a skillet over medium–high heat. Add as many chicken breasts as will fit in the skillet in a single layer and cook on each side for 2 minutes, or until the chicken is golden, cooked through, and there is no sign of pink or red when cut through with a knife. Cook the remaining chicken, adding extra oil, if necessary.

5. Pour half of the sauce into a baking dish that will hold the chicken in a single layer. Arrange the chicken on top, then drizzle with the remaining sauce. Arrange the mozzarella on top and sprinkle with the Parmesan. Bake in the preheated oven for 20–25 minutes, or until the cheese is melted, golden, and bubbling. Let stand for 5 minutes, then garnish with parsley. Serve immediately.

CHICKEN & WILD MUSHROOM CANNELLONI

SERVES: 4   **PREP TIME: 20 MINS**   **COOK TIME: 1 HR 50 MINS**

INGREDIENTS

butter, for greasing
2 tablespoons olive oil
2 garlic cloves, crushed
1 large onion, finely chopped
8 ounces wild mushrooms sliced
12 ounces ground chicken
4 ounces prosciutto, diced
⅔ cup red wine
¾ cup canned diced tomatoes
1 tablespoon shredded fresh basil leaves
2 tablespoons tomato paste
10–12 dried cannelloni tubes
2½ cups white sauce
1 cup freshly grated Parmesan cheese
salt and pepper, to taste

1. Preheat the oven to 375°F. Lightly grease a large ovenproof dish. Heat the olive oil in a heavy skillet. Add the garlic, onion, and mushrooms and cook over low heat, stirring frequently, for 8–10 minutes. Add the chicken and prosciutto and cook, stirring frequently, for 12 minutes, or until browned. Stir in the red wine, tomatoes, basil, and tomato paste and cook for 4 minutes. Season with salt and pepper, then cover and simmer for 30 minutes. Uncover, stir, and simmer for 15 minutes.

2. Meanwhile, bring a large, heavy saucepan of lightly salted water to a boil. Add the cannelloni, bring back to a boil, and cook for 8–10 minutes, or according to package directions, until just tender but still firm to the bite. Using a slotted spoon, transfer to a plate and pat dry.

3. Using a teaspoon, fill the cannelloni tubes with the chicken-and-mushroom mixture. Transfer to the dish. Pour the white sauce over them to cover completely and sprinkle with the Parmesan cheese.

4. Bake in the preheated oven for 30 minutes, or until golden brown and bubbling. Serve immediately.

BUTTERFLIED CHICKEN WITH LEMON & HONEY

SERVES: 4

PREP TIME: 10 MINS PLUS MARINATING

COOK TIME: 45–55 MINS

INGREDIENTS

2 tablespoons honey

1 tablespoon freshly squeezed lemon juice

¼ teaspoon hot or sweet paprika, to taste

1 (3¼-pound) chicken, butterflied

sunflower oil, for oiling

salt and pepper, to taste

finely chopped fresh flat-leaf parsley and finely grated lemon rind, to garnish

1. Mix together the honey, lemon juice, and paprika in a wide, nonmetallic bowl large enough to hold the chicken flat, and season with salt and pepper.

2. Add the chicken and rub in the mixture all over, then let stand for 30 minutes at room temperature.

3. Meanwhile, preheat the oven to 375°F. Put a greased rack into a roasting pan large enough to hold the chicken flat.

4. When ready to cook, oil two long metal skewers. Place the chicken on a cutting board and run the skewers through the body in an X shape.

5. Place the chicken on the prepared rack, skin-side up, and brush with the marinade. Roast in the preheated oven for 45–55 minutes, brushing with the marinade twice, until a meat thermometer reads 180°F, or until the skin is golden brown and the juices run clear when the thickest part of the meat is pierced with the tip of a sharp knife.

6. Remove from the oven, cover with aluminum foil, and let rest for 5 minutes. Use a metal spoon to skim the fat off the pan juices. Carve the chicken, spoon the pan juices over it, and garnish with the parsley and lemon rind.

4

2

5

HIT THE SAUCE!

A fresh whole chicken or chicken parts can be marinated before cooking to tenderize the flesh and add flavor and moisture. Rubs can also be used to season the chicken before cooking, and many different sauces can be cooked or served with chicken to add extra flavor. The following quick-and-easy recipes give examples of a marinade, rub, and sauce, all of which are suitable for chicken.

When roasting a whole chicken, you can also add flavor to the meat in several simple ways:

• Put a whole lemon or small orange (pierced a couple of times), a peeled onion, or a few sprigs of fresh herbs and peeled garlic cloves inside the cavity of the bird before roasting.

• Gently insert citrus fruit slices (lemon or orange are ideal) or fresh herb sprigs (thyme, rosemary, or marjoram work well) under the skin covering the breast, before roasting.

• Carefully spread a flavored butter (such as garlic or herb butter) under the skin covering the breast before roasting.

• Brush the outside of a whole chicken with oil, then sprinkle with ground spices or a spice seasoning mix, or dried herbs or a mixed herb seasoning of your choice, to add extra flavor and color.

STICKY BARBECUE MARINADE

This tasty marinade cooks to a gloriously sticky, flavorsome coating and is especially good with chicken.

Makes enough for about 1 pound of chicken parts

¼ cup firmly packed light or dark brown sugar
⅓ cup plum preserves
2 tablespoons tomato paste
2 tablespoons white wine vinegar
1 tablespoon whole-grain mustard

1. Heat all the ingredients together in a saucepan over low heat, stirring until smooth. Remove from the heat and let cool.

2. Score the chicken parts deeply with a sharp knife. Put the prepared chicken in a shallow, nonmetallic dish or plastic food bag.

3. Pour the cold marinade over the prepared chicken and turn to coat all over. Cover tightly or seal and marinate in the refrigerator, turning occasionally, for at least 1 hour or preferably overnight, before cooking.

Hero Tips
• Try using other types of preserves, such as apricot preserves, or marmalade, in place of the plum preserves.

• Marinade that has been used to marinate raw chicken should not be used on cooked chicken, nor should it be used to baste chicken during cooking, especially toward the end of the cooking time.

CAJUN BLACKENED SPICE RUB
Use this tasty rub to add flavor to chicken pieces before cooking.

Makes about ¼ cup
1 tablespoon cracked black peppercorns
2 teaspoons paprika
2 teaspoons garlic powder or crushed garlic
2 teaspoons salt
1 teaspoon dried thyme
1 teaspoon dried oregano
1 teaspoon mustard powder
½ teaspoon cayenne pepper

1. Mix all the ingredients together in a small bowl until thoroughly combined.

2. Rub the spice mixture thoroughly into the chicken, just before cooking if short of time, or preferably several hours before cooking.

3. Put the prepared chicken in a shallow dish, cover tightly, and chill in the refrigerator until you are ready to cook it.

SATAY SAUCE
Satay sauce is a tasty accompaniment or dip for grilled or barbecued chicken kebabs, chicken pieces, or chicken satay skewers.

Makes about 1 cup
4 scallions, coarsely chopped
1 garlic clove, coarsely chopped
2 teaspoons chopped fresh ginger
⅓ cup peanut butter
1 teaspoon packed light brown sugar
1 teaspoon Thai fish sauce
2 tablespoons soy sauce
1 tablespoon chili sauce or Tabasco sauce
1 teaspoon lemon juice
salt, to taste
peanuts, to garnish

1. Put all the ingredients into a food processor. Add ⅔ cup water and process to a puree.

2. Transfer to a saucepan, season with salt, and heat gently, stirring occasionally. Transfer to a bowl and sprinkle with the peanuts to garnish. Serve warm or cold.

CHICKEN BASQUAISE

SERVES: 4

PREP TIME: 10 MINS

COOK TIME: 1 HR 20 MINS

INGREDIENTS

2 tablespoons all-purpose flour

1 (3-pound) chicken, cut into 8 parts

3 tablespoons olive oil

1 Bermuda onion, thickly sliced

2 red or yellow bell peppers, seeded and cut into thick strips

2 garlic cloves

6 ounces chorizo sausage, cut into ½-inch pieces

1 tablespoon tomato paste

1 cup long-grain rice

2 cups chicken stock

1 teaspoon crushed red pepper flakes

½ teaspoon dried thyme

4 ounces prosciutto, diced

12 dry-cured black ripe olives

salt and pepper, to taste

chopped fresh flat-leaf parsley, to garnish

1. Put the flour in a plastic bag and season well with salt and pepper. Add the chicken to the bag, tie the top, and shake well to coat. Heat 2 tablespoons of the oil in a large Dutch oven or saucepan over medium–high heat. Add the chicken and cook, turning frequently, for about 15 minutes, until browned all over. Transfer to a plate.

2. Heat the remaining oil in the pan and add the onion and bell peppers. Reduce the heat to medium and sauté until beginning to brown and soften. Add the garlic, chorizo, and tomato paste and cook, stirring constantly, for about 3 minutes. Add the rice and cook, stirring to coat, for about 2 minutes, until the grains are translucent.

3. Add the stock, red pepper flakes, and thyme to the pan. Season with salt and pepper. Stir well and bring to a boil, then return the chicken to the pan, pressing it gently into the rice. Cover and cook over low heat for about 45 minutes, until the rice is tender and the chicken juices run clear when the tip of a sharp knife is inserted into the thickest part of the meat.

4. Gently stir the prosciutto and olives into the rice mixture. Replace the lid and heat through for an additional 5 minutes. Garnish with parsley and serve immediately.

COQ AU VIN

This rich Burgundian stew was once the farmhouse cook's modest way of tenderizing and flavoring tough old birds. Today, however, it must be one of France's best-loved and well-known dishes.

SERVES: 4 **PREP TIME: 10 MINS** **COOK TIME: APPROX. 1 HR 20 MINS**

INGREDIENTS

4 tablespoons butter
2 tablespoons olive oil
4 pounds chicken parts
4 ounces bacon, cut into strips
4 ounces pearl onions
4 ounces cremini mushrooms, halved
2 garlic cloves, finely chopped
2 tablespoons brandy
1 cup red wine
1¼ cups chicken stock
1 bouquet garni of sprigs of parsley, thyme, and bay leaf tied together
2 tablespoons all-purpose flour
salt and pepper, to taste
bay leaves, to garnish

1. Melt half the butter with the oil in a large Dutch oven or saucepan. Add the chicken and cook over medium heat, stirring, for 8–10 minutes, or until browned all over. Add the bacon, onions, mushrooms, and garlic.

2. Pour in the brandy and set it alight with a match or taper. When the flames have died down, add the wine, stock, and bouquet garni and season with salt and pepper. Bring to a boil, reduce the heat, and simmer gently for 1 hour, or until the chicken is tender and the juices run clear when the tip of a sharp knife is inserted into the thickest part of the meat.

3. Remove and discard the bouquet garni. Transfer the chicken to a large plate and keep warm. Mix the flour with the remaining butter and whisk the butter paste into the pan, a little at a time. Bring to a boil, return the chicken to the pan, and heat through. Garnish with bay leaves and serve immediately (do not eat the bay leaves).

CHICKEN GUMBO

SERVES: 4–6   **PREP TIME: 30 MINS**   **COOK TIME: 2½ HRS**

INGREDIENTS

1 (3¼-pound) chicken, cut into 6 parts

2 celery stalks, 1 broken in half and 1 finely chopped

1 carrot, chopped

2 onions, 1 sliced and 1 chopped

2 bay leaves

¼ teaspoon salt

¼ cup canola oil or peanut oil

⅓ cup all-purpose flour

2 large garlic cloves, crushed

1 green bell pepper, cored, seeded, and diced

1 pound fresh okra, cut crosswise into ½-inch slices

8 ounces andouille sausage or Polish kielbasa, sliced

2 tablespoons tomato paste

1 teaspoon dried thyme

½ teaspoon salt

½ teaspoon cayenne pepper

¼ teaspoon pepper

1 (14½-ounce) can plum tomatoes

cooked long-grain rice and hot pepper sauce, to serve

1. Put the chicken into a large saucepan with enough water to cover over medium–high heat and bring to a boil, skimming the surface to remove the foam. When the foam stops rising, reduce the heat to medium, add the celery stalk halves, carrot, sliced onion, 1 bay leaf, and salt and simmer for 20 minutes, or until the chicken is tender and the juices run clear when the tip of a sharp knife is inserted into the thickest part of the meat. Strain the chicken, reserving 4 cups of the liquid. When the chicken is cool enough to handle, remove and discard the skin, bones, and flavorings. Cut the meat into bite-size pieces and reserve.

2. Heat the oil in a large saucepan over medium–high heat for 2 minutes. Reduce the heat to low, sprinkle in the flour, and stir to make a paste. Stir constantly for around 20 minutes, or until the paste turns hazelnut brown. If black specks appear, it is burned and you will have to start again.

3. Add the chopped celery, chopped onion, garlic, green bell pepper, and okra to the saucepan. Increase the heat to medium–high and cook, stirring frequently, for 5 minutes. Add the sausage and cook, stirring frequently, for 2 minutes.

4. Stir in the remaining ingredients, including the second bay leaf and the reserved cooking liquid. Bring to a boil, crushing the tomatoes with a wooden spoon. Reduce the heat to low–medium and simmer, uncovered, for 30 minutes, stirring occasionally.

5. Add the chicken to the pan and simmer for another 30 minutes. Taste and adjust the seasoning, if necessary. Remove and discard the bay leaves and spoon the gumbo over the rice. Serve with a bottle of hot pepper sauce on the side.

BAKED CHICKEN & CHORIZO PAELLA

SERVES: 4　　　　**PREP TIME: 20 MINS**　　　**COOK TIME: 40–45 MINS**

INGREDIENTS

2 tablespoons olive oil

4 ounces chorizo sausages, skinned and sliced

1 onion, finely chopped

1 red bell pepper, seeded and coarsely chopped

1 pound boneless, skinless chicken thighs, cut into bite-size pieces

4 large garlic cloves, finely chopped

1¾ cups paella or risotto rice

1 cup frozen peas

1 teaspoon Spanish sweet paprika

large pinch of saffron threads

½ cup dry white wine

3 cups chicken stock or vegetable stock

8 ounces large raw shrimp, peeled and deveined

salt and pepper, to taste

chopped fresh flat-leaf parsley, to garnish

lemon wedges, to serve

1. Preheat the oven to 425°F. Heat the oil in a large Dutch oven or flameproof casserole dish over high heat. Reduce the heat to low–medium, add the chorizo, and cook, stirring, for 3–4 minutes, until it starts to brown and release its oil. Remove from the pan and pour off all but 2 tablespoons of the oil.

2. Add the onion and red bell pepper and sauté, stirring, for 3–5 minutes, until soft. Add the chicken and garlic and stir until the meat is browned all over.

3. Add the rice and peas, gently stirring until the rice is coated in oil. Stir in the paprika and saffron threads, then add the wine and stock and season with salt and pepper. Bring to a boil, stirring occasionally, then transfer to the preheated oven and bake, uncovered, for 15 minutes.

4. Remove from the oven and add the shrimp and chorizo, pushing them down into the rice. Return to the oven and bake for an additional 10 minutes, or until the rice is tender, the prawns are pink and cooked through, and the chicken is done. Cut into the middle of the chicken to check there are no remaining traces of pink or red. Garnish with parsley and serve with lemon wedges.

JAMBALAYA

SERVES: 4

PREP TIME: 25 MINS

COOK TIME: APPROX. 45 MINS

INGREDIENTS

2 tablespoons vegetable oil

2 onions, coarsely chopped

1 green bell pepper, seeded and coarsely chopped

2 celery stalks, coarsely chopped

3 garlic cloves, finely chopped

2 teaspoons paprika

10 ounces skinless, boneless chicken breasts, chopped

4 ounces kabanos sausages, chopped

3 tomatoes, peeled and chopped

2¼ cups long-grain rice

3½ cups chicken stock or fish stock

1 teaspoon dried oregano

2 bay leaves

12 large raw shrimp, peeled and deveined

4 scallions, finely chopped

salt and pepper, to taste

chopped fresh flat-leaf parsley, to garnish

1. Heat the oil in a large skillet over low heat. Add the onions, green bell pepper, celery, and garlic and cook for 8–10 minutes. Stir in the paprika and cook for an additional 30 seconds. Add the chicken and sausages and cook for 8–10 minutes, until lightly browned. Add the tomatoes and cook for 2–3 minutes.

2. Add the rice to the skillet and stir well. Pour in the stock, oregano, and bay leaves and stir well. Cover and simmer for 10 minutes.

3. Add the shrimp and stir. Replace the lid and cook for an additional 6–8 minutes, until the rice is tender and the chicken and shrimp are cooked through. To check the chicken is cooked through, cut into the middle to check there are no remaining traces of pink or red. Remove and discard the bay leaves. Stir in the scallions and season with salt and pepper. Garnish with parsley and serve immediately.

CHICKEN CASSEROLE WITH A HERB CRUST

SERVES: 4

PREP TIME: 15 MINS

COOK TIME: 1 HR 40 MINS

INGREDIENTS

4 chicken legs
2 tablespoons all-purpose flour
1 tablespoon butter
1 tablespoon olive oil
1 onion, chopped
3 garlic cloves, sliced
4 parsnips, cut into large chunks
⅔ cup dry white wine
3½ cups chicken stock
3 leeks, white parts only, sliced
8 prunes, halved (optional)
1 tablespoon English mustard
1 bouquet garni
2 cups fresh bread crumbs
⅔ cup shredded Manchego, Monterey Jack, or cheddar cheese
¾ cup mixed fresh tarragon and flat-leaf parsley, chopped
salt and pepper, to taste

1. Preheat the oven to 350°F. Toss the chicken legs in the flour, shaking off any excess. Melt the butter with the oil in a large Dutch oven or flameproof casserole dish. Add the chicken and cook, turning occasionally, until golden brown all over. Remove with a slotted spoon and keep warm.

2. Add the onion, garlic, and parsnips to the pan and cook for 20 minutes, or until the mixture is golden brown.

3. Add the wine, stock, leeks, prunes (if using), mustard, and bouquet garni and season with salt and pepper.

4. Return the chicken to the pan, cover, and cook in the preheated oven for 1 hour. Meanwhile, mix together the bread crumbs, cheese, and herbs.

5. Remove the pan from the oven and increase the temperature to 400°F.

6. Remove the lid of the pan and sprinkle with the crust mixture. Return the casserole to the oven, uncovered, for 10 minutes, until the crust starts to brown slightly, the chicken is cooked through, and the juices run clear when the tip of a sharp knife is inserted into the thickest part of the meat. Serve immediately.

SWEET CHILI CHICKEN WITH CREOLE RICE

SERVES: 4

PREP TIME: 15 MINS PLUS MARINATING

COOK TIME: APPROX. 45 MINS

INGREDIENTS

8 skinless, boneless chicken thighs, about 4 ounces each

2 tablespoons sweet chili sauce

2 tablespoons orange juice

2 garlic cloves, crushed

salt and pepper, to taste

CREOLE RICE

2½ cups water

1¼ cups long-grain rice

1 tablespoon olive oil

1 large red bell pepper, seeded and finely chopped

1 small onion, finely chopped

1 teaspoon paprika

2 cups rinsed and drained mixed beans, such as kidney beans, pinto beans, and chickpeas

1. Put the chicken thighs in a shallow, nonmetallic bowl. Mix together the chili sauce, orange juice, and garlic in a small bowl, season with a little salt and pepper, and spoon over the chicken. Turn the chicken to coat thoroughly in the marinade. Cover and let marinate in the refrigerator for 1–2 hours.

2. Preheat the oven to 350°F. Transfer the chicken thighs to a nonstick baking pan and bake in the preheated oven, turning halfway through, for 25 minutes, or until tender and the juices run clear when the tip of a sharp knife is inserted into the thickest part of the meat.

3. Meanwhile, make the creole rice. Pour the water into a saucepan, add a little salt, and bring to a boil. Add the rice and stir well. Cover, reduce the heat to low and let simmer, undisturbed for 15 minutes, or according to package directions, until tender.

4. Heat the oil in a saucepan over medium–high heat, add the red bell pepper and onion, and cook, stirring frequently, for 10–15 minutes, until the onion is soft, adding the paprika in the last 5 minutes of the cooking time. Stir in the beans and cook for an additional minute.

5. Stir the bean mixture into the cooked rice. Transfer to plates and top with the chicken. Serve immediately.

CHICKEN WITH FORTY CLOVES OF GARLIC

SERVES: 6　　　　**PREP TIME: 10 MINS**　　　**COOK TIME: 1½–1¾ HRS**

INGREDIENTS

1 (3½-pound) chicken

3 garlic bulbs, separated into cloves but unpeeled

6 fresh thyme sprigs

2 fresh tarragon sprigs

2 bay leaves

1¼ cups dry white wine

salt and pepper, to taste

1. Preheat the oven to 350°F. Season the chicken inside and out with salt and pepper, then truss with kitchen string. Place on a rack in a Dutch oven or flameproof casserole dish and arrange the garlic and herbs around it.

2. Pour the wine over the chicken and cover with a tight-fitting lid. Cook in the preheated oven for 1½ –1¾ hours, until a meat thermometer reads 180°F, or until the chicken is tender and the juices run clear when the tip of a sharp knife is inserted into the thickest part of the meat.

3. Remove and discard the bay leaves. Transfer the chicken and garlic to a dish and keep warm. Strain the cooking juices into a small bowl. Skim off any fat on the surface of the cooking juices.

4. Carve the chicken and transfer to serving plates with the garlic. Spoon over a little of the cooking juices and serve immediately.

HERO TIPS

If you find that the garlic is browning much quicker than the chicken, simply remove from the dish with a slotted spoon and set aside. You can then add them back into the dish a short while before the chicken is ready, to warm back through.

INDEX